Arsenal Services Ltd and Stallion Enterprises International Corporation

OPERATION: JOB SEARCH

Your comprehensive and tactical guide to securing the ultimate job

Josh Arsenault and Andrew Soave
First Edition | Winter 2018

MISSION OVERVIEW:

Use this space to write in your motivations for taking this course and for finding a new job.

The Recruitment "Game"

Recruitment is a game – a search conducted by two parties to determine if there is a value fit. As the Job Seeker, you find value in securing work that will sustain you and that you are proud of. The Recruiter finds value in hiring quality candidates.

How the Recruiter Thinks

Think about the last job you had, or even the next job you are going to take. Do you want to be a top performer, or will you settle for being at the bottom of the list? If you're like most people, you'd much rather be performing well, and would hate for your boss to tell you that you've done something wrong at work. Negative feedback is difficult for many of us to receive.

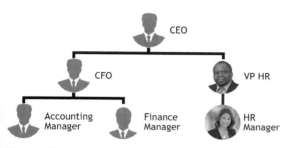

Hiring Managers are no different. They have a manager to report to, and they have performance reviews just like everyone else. When they hire strong candidates, they may receive positive feedback from their company. When they hire weak candidates, though, they will almost always receive negative feedback. These payoffs are viewed as a slight positive payoff and a significant negative payoff, respectively, and together they discourage hiring "risky" candidates.

Therefore, most Hiring Managers are risk-averse: they hire "safe" candidates. Safe candidates are capable of doing their work, able to work independently, and are friendly and interesting to others. Put simply, these candidates demonstrate high value.

This booklet will focus on demonstrating high value as a key objective throughout your job search; however, a job seeker can become a "safe hire" through referrals as well:

- A referral from upper management is a safe hire for the recruiter because the hire has been requested by someone else. When the recruiter adheres to a manager's request and the candidate fails, the recruiter is not to blame, and therefore is not at risk.
- A referral from an employee within the company also takes some of the risk from the recruiter, and the recruiter's perceived risk depends on the tenure and performance of that employee.
- A referral through the recruiter's personal contacts reduces the perceived risk to the recruiter, and this reduction depends on the trust they have for their counterpart.

Note that in any of these situations, you must demonstrate high value as a candidate to be referred, which makes this skill the most critical throughout your job search.

Three Pillars of Candidate Value
Candidate Value is split into three main aspects of roughly equal importance. Each aspect is necessary but not sufficient; that is, a high-value candidate must demonstrate each of these to some degree in order to be successful.

Competence - you are willing and able to do the work
The first aspect is obvious – you need some degree of skill to do the work. You must also be willing to put in the hours and effort needed to get everything done when asked. Competence is largely demonstrated by your accomplishments, usually those that relate to school or work, and sometimes less formal instances, such as organizing an event for friends, or volunteering. Your competence is your ability to solve problems and create value for others; creating more than you consume.

Confidence - you take initiative and demonstrate leadership
Your ability is nothing without action, and confidence is how you make things happen. Confidence is the initiative that allows you to take control of a situation, lead others, and bring the desired future into existence. A confident person is able to express themselves, both when they want something from others, and when they are unsure of a situation. Confidence is built from awareness of the self and the situation, both of which are developed in this program.

Interest - you are interesting and get along well with others
The last aspect is the most underrated. Research shows the importance of being friendly, welcoming and interesting in both professional and personal relationships. Since the recruitment process is often ineffective, most stakeholders rely on "senses" and "feelings" when judging a candidate. This presents a significant loophole for savvy job seekers to leverage. An interesting person has fun and exciting stories about the different things they do or have done in the past, and they are memorable to everyone in the room. A person develops interest not by lavish trips or elite skill, but through creating adventure in their own life, being open to new experiences, and by demonstrating a positive attitude through all situations.

Exercise 1: Reflect on Your Candidate Value
The three pillars – Competence, Confidence, and Interest – form the CCI model of candidate value, and are critical in your recruitment journey as they are in any other relationship. Before moving to the next chapter, check your understanding by evaluating your value as a candidate:

What problems do I solve? What do I create? Do I create more than I consume?

In which situations do I hesitate from taking action? What consequences am I afraid of?

What do I do that others find interesting? How can I eliminate negativity from my life?

What aspect of candidate value do I demonstrate best? What do I need to work on?

Start from Within

Before you start calling employers, understand your goals and where you stand in relation to them. We'll be working with specific goals, as opposed to simply "finding a job". The combination of skills that you have position you for a specific type of work; therefore, you must understand which type of work you are suited for, and be able to explain why. This level of self-awareness demonstrates both competence and confidence to the recruiter.

Clarify Your Goals

Remember when you were younger, and adults asked you, "what do you want to be when you grow up"? Your answer was "a doctor", "an astronaut", "the president", or perhaps something more common. Either way, the question leads us to an ineffective answer: we focused on what we wanted to be, not on what we wanted to do. As a result, most job-seekers limit their search by job titles, not by the problems that they want to solve. In many roles, employees work on tasks that are out of scope of their true function, and many job postings feature a vague job description that often isn't reflective of the work the employee will actually do.

Instead, we'll ask ourselves, "what problems do I want to solve?" which unlocks many opportunities you would never have thought of otherwise. More importantly, every role on this revised list will be one you are passionate about.

Exercise 2: Be at Your Best

Values are the personal principles or standards we hold. Each person's values inform them of the type of workplace they thrive in, and those situations where they "fit". Understanding our own values helps us to therefore determine the environments in which we can be most successful. This exercise will prompt you to think about what is most important in your life.

Identify three defining experiences in your life where you were at your best.

1.

2.

3.

Consider the following questions as you look for similarities in these experiences:

- Were you alone or in a group?
- What type of challenge did you face?
- How did you overcome the challenge?
- What skills did you use?
- What are you proud of, and why was this a defining moment?

Now identify three common themes about these experiences. Examples may include "taking risks", "persistence", or "leading a team".

To perform your best in the future, the work environment must facilitate your values. Using the themes above, what do you need from your job to perform your best?

Example: if you identified "taking risks", your future position would provide you with the ability to make decisions on your own, and a safe space to make mistakes.

Exercise 3: Love Your Work
Sadly, most people think of work as, well, work. They dread the start of their day, they long for time off, and they are unhappy at work and at home. Not every interest can become a full-time gig, but enjoying work is a necessary factor for success and satisfaction. The questions on the next page can guide what you are really interested in.

You are in your ideal future job. What does your business card say? What are the functions of the role that you enjoy most? What makes you successful in it? Where is this job?

You just won on a CASH FOR LIFE scratch card. You'll still need to work to maintain some savings, but with an extra $1,000 every week, your paycheque is irrelevant. What roles or initiatives would be the most enjoyable for you? Why are they more enjoyable than others? What aspects of the work environment satisfy you? What does your life look like now?

What themes or aspects of these answers can be applied to your career path?

Define Your Goals

Notice that the last two sections focus on inputs: the activities that you do each day and the environment that you work in. These sections demonstrate the foundations of goal-based searching, as opposed to label-based searching. Now take this further, and see how much more powerful goal-based searching is than label-based searching. First, write down a target role – ideally a job title – in the space below.

Exercise 4: Clarifying Your Goals

For the job title above, list three tasks or initiatives that excite you while doing this job. We'll call these "role goals":

1.

2.

3.

Now, for each of the three role goals above, list five other roles in which you could accomplish that specific role goal. List jobs in different functions and industries whenever possible. You may find that the same alternate job applies to more than one role goal.

	Role Goal 1	Role Goal 2	Role Goal 3
Alternate 1			
Alternate 2			
Alternate 3			
Alternate 4			
Alternate 5			

Each position listed above is an alternative path to reaching your goals. Search each of these positions on LinkedIn, one at a time. The results will include LinkedIn users with the role you searched and might include some job postings. Either way, you can use these profiles and postings to find companies in which the role is part of the organizational structure. Use the first 25 companies you see in each search to create combinations of positions and companies that you can list in your "My Targets and Tracking" sheet in the OPERATION: JOB SEARCH Tools Package.

You will now have over 100 combinations for potential target companies. No matter how effective your job search becomes, quantity yields more opportunities and therefore more bargaining power.

Of course, this list provides a starting point. The most effective job seekers will find more opportunities as they learn to network at every opportunity, and cold-call the employers that interest them. In any case, you've now created a list of options that not only increases the number of opportunities available to you but also focuses you on a subset of all of the opportunities out there. Later, you'll see how to contact people for each of these opportunities.

Identify Your Strengths

Your leverage as a candidate is directly dependent on the recruiter's expectation of the value you will contribute to the company in your future role. This expected value is maximized under three conditions:

1. The type of work matches your personal strengths
2. The type of work is performed better by you than by others
3. Sufficient evidence exists to support both of the above statements

Remember, the recruiter's incentive is to make safe hires. Therefore, they will be looking to your past performance to predict future performance. Of course, it's not enough to say that you have skills without any proof.

Exercise 5: What Can I Do?
Start this exercise by reflecting on your last three years, which is typically a combination of school and work for most readers. Use the cues and spaces below to write your accomplishments.

What businesses or initiatives have you been a part of in the last three years? What major accomplishments have these entities had? How did you contribute?

How have you created value at work or in a business in a way that others did not?

What difficult situations or conversations did you need to navigate?

When have you done something outside your role at work?

If you were in school, what did you do when you weren't in class?

Did you contribute to extracurricular sports, clubs, or groups? What accomplishments did these organizations have that you were a part of?

In your extracurriculars or team-based projects, when did you lead the team through an initiative or setback?

What courses did you take during school? What were the tangible and valuable outputs of the projects you had for these courses?

What new skills did you learn with the courses you took?

What events or initiatives have you volunteered to help in?

Did you plan or assist with social events, either as part of an organization or informally with a large group of friends?

Use this list of accomplishments to write down 10 – 25 specific skills or strengths that you have, as demonstrated by the accomplishments. Examples may include subject matter ("marketing"), skills ("programming"), or specific qualities ("motivating others").

What are the common themes in the list above? Choose 3 – 5 themes that capture the ideas in this list. These themes can be single words, but they can also be larger phrases or ideas.

Using these themes, build a personal brand statement in two sentences. This statement will should feel like an elevator pitch and explain how you bring value to organizations.

"I realize value in organizations by assessing operations and helping managers implement solutions to improve their process and systems. I align operations with marketing, strategy, and talent to create high-performing organizations."

Driving Value in a Business

Most of the skills and brand statements above will only have a limited value to the business. For this reason, read *The Small Business Booklet* and select three sections that you feel confident in, or that are related to skills you listed above. Consider these as additional skills.

Using your answers above and in the last section, rewrite your brand statement, making sure that you explain how your skills create business value. Keep your brand statement under 40 words.

Polish your Profiles

In almost every recruitment path, your resume or LinkedIn profile will be analyzed by the recruiter. Before you create the connections that will lead to recruitment paths, you should have all your documents ready.

Resume

Your resume is your master document for recruitment. It will include most, if not all, of your accomplishments until you are at least 25. Since most people only scan a resume, the format and layout of the resume is more important than the individual points, and as a job seeker you want to avoid creating "red flags" more than trying to sell your expertise – your conversations will yield better opportunities to demonstrate your value.

A sample resume is shown to the right, using the template available in the *OJS – Word Document Templates* File. Create your resume using the instructions below:

1. Begin with your name in bold, as well as your contact information below. Add your LinkedIn URL and ensure that it is personalized to your name.

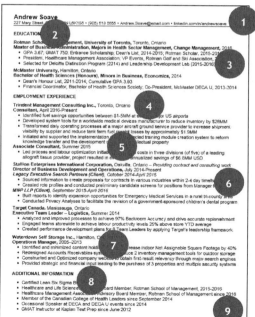

2. Sections should be in the following order for all students or recent graduates: Education, Experience, Additional Information. Those without education or with over ten years of post-graduation experience may choose to reorder these sections. All sections should have a blank space above and below them, and be bolded or capitalized so that they stand out for easy navigation.

3. If you have a strong GPA or received other awards, include them in the top bullet. Then list all initiatives you participated in, grouping related information on the same line if needed. Where you participated in something that required an application, use the term "selected" instead of "member" or "participated". If you had a notable accomplishment in any of these activities, you can add it here.

4. Employment is listed with the most recent first. Use bullet points to list real accomplishments where you brought value to an organization, and ensure that at least half of your bullet points have a number or other quantifiable value: preferably a dollar value. Begin each bullet point with an action verb that puts you in control: for example, "initiated and supported" is stronger than "facilitated".

5. If you had multiple positions at the same organization, include the other title to save space. You can also use this technique if you had multiple clients and can share their names. Separate all employers with a space to help the headings stand out.

6. Include freelance work if you have one or more accomplishment to include in this heading. You should include a description, italicized, after the name for any organization in which the company's work is not easily understood.

7. Avoid using the specific months of your employment if you held a position for less than six months. You can also exclude months if you worked at a position for more than 3 years continuously.

8. Add additional information including other accomplishments, certifications, or memberships. You can also use this space for any jobs you've had that are informal (e.g. tutoring or babysitting), irrelevant based on the accomplishments in that job (e.g. speaking engagements), or have too few accomplishments to put in an earlier section (e.g. freelance work).

9. The resume should be one page, at least three-quarters full, without exception. Use margins, fonts, and spaces to reach this range, and change content if necessary. Reword any bullet that does not use one or two full lines on the page. The page should have justified te (icon) and the file saved as a PDF in the following format: [NAME] – Resume – YYMMDD. Use [Last, First] for your name if your last name is alphabetically higher than your first.

For example, Josh Arsenault would use "Arsenault, Josh – Resume – 170115" for a Resume dated January 15th, 2017.

LinkedIn Profile

Your LinkedIn profile has the potential to help you create new connections but only when you do both of the following:

1. You maintain a complete, accurate, and navigable profile that showcases your talent
2. You actively share content on a regular basis that draws the attention of others

Regardless of whether you already have a LinkedIn profile, follow these steps to ensure your profile is useful to your job search. Use the pictures to guide you through these steps:

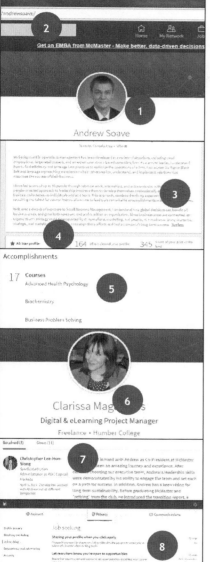

1. Begin by personalizing your LinkedIn URL to your name or initials. If you must use numbers, use a single digit number, or your graduation date (two or four digits). Do not use your birth year.

2. Choose a profile picture that has a simple background and only includes your face and shoulders, wearing formal clothing. Have a friend take this picture for you if you do not have one. If you choose to have a background photo, keep it very simple.

3. Write a summary of one to three paragraphs summarizing your accomplishments according to your resume, as well as your interests. Write the summary in the first-person and do not include that you are looking for opportunities.

4. Complete all the sections of your profile until you have an "All-Star Profile". This indicates that your profile is complete. Almost all sections can be replicated from your resume and maintain the same bullet point format for each position.

5. List all courses that are relevant to the functions or industries of your target companies. Ensure the courses are listed in alphabetical order for clarity.

6. Include freelance work as one of your current positions, and er   title of the role matches with your aspirations. List the employer as "Freelance" or use the name of a personal company if you have one. Use this position title as your LinkedIn headline. Ensure you have a description to the position: at a minimum, use "Providing contract-based work to clients." and list specialities based on the relevant skills you listed in the previous section.

7. Ask for recommendations from anyone that you have worked with, including friends or professors. Aim to have at least five on your profile.

8. Finally, click on your profile's settings, and go to the "Privacy" menu. Under "Job Seeking", in the option "Let recruiters know you're open to opportunities", select "yes" and update all career interests to match your "My Targets and Tracking" sheet in the OPERATION: JOB SEARCH Tools Package.

Once you have built a complete LinkedIn profile, you attract people to the profile by creating and sharing valuable content. Remember, a Competent candidate creates more than they consume, and therefore you will not be noticed by simply liking the content of others. Use the following as a minimum standard during your job search:

- Make a thoughtful comment on one post or update every day
- Share one post or article every day, ideally related to your target companies
- Write and share one article every month that you created yourself

Building Connections

At this point, you have built a strong list of target positions and have most of the self-awareness that will be useful for your search. The additional awareness comes with time and practice – and practice can only be gained through making connections. You will want to connect with many new people and companies each day to maximize the number of recruitment paths you are exposed at once. Additional paths will provide more practice and more opportunities, both of which increase your chances of finding your next job. There are two methods by which to make connections, each of which is useful in different situations.

Cold Calling

This method of making connections is commonly associated with sales, and if done properly, cold calls (or emails) can be effective. A "cold call" is a term for reaching out without any introduction, generally for a specific purpose. In this age of recruitment, a well-executed cold call demonstrates exceptionally high confidence, and, given that it is more prominent in higher levels of Executive Search, it will yield the perception of competence. Most importantly, a cold call catches the attention of the recruiter immediately, because it requires their effort and additional thinking, which most applications fail to do.

There are two primary reasons why you would cold call:

1. You are seeking a mentor or sponsor
2. You are seeking employment

These two reasons have similar objectives but different approaches. However, both types of call or email require that you demonstrate high value to catch the target's attention.

For Mentorship

When asking for mentorship, keep a keen eye for what the target considers themselves an expert in, as this should form the basis of the connection. Relate their expertise to something you have worked on, or plan to do in the future, and include a simple but thought-out question for them to answer. A sample email is found in the "Mentorship Cold Call" sheet in the OPERATION: JOB SEARCH Tools Package.

The sample email demonstrates the fundamental aspects of the Mentorship Cold Call. First, you must show an understanding of someone's work to demonstrate your appreciation for it. Second, you've demonstrating value through your expertise in a similar subject. Third, you specified an ask that creates a reason for the target to respond. Finally, you have demonstrated confidence in the final lines of the email that you expect a response and will follow-up.

Exercise 6: Cold Calling (Part 1)

Practice writing one email each to CEOs of companies on your target list or celebrities that you admire.

Target 1 Email:

Target 2 Email:

For Employment

More commonly, you will be contacting recruiters to find work, either in response to a posting or to discover opportunities that aren't posted. In this scenario, demonstrate your value in a relevant way by talking about your past experiences as they relate to the role. In this email, show not only interest in the role or company, but also alternatives: demonstrating choice increases the recruiter's perception of your value.

Two sample emails are found in in the OPERATION: JOB SEARCH Tools Package. When responding to a posting, the cold call should be addressed to the recruiter whenever possible, but do not attach a resume. In contrast, emails used to discover opportunities should be sent to the highest-ranking managers you can find the contact information for. In larger companies, you could send this email to several different contacts in different departments and at different levels.

Exercise 7: Cold Calling (Part 2)

To practice, write one of each type of email in the spaces below. Address the emails to two of the targets on your list.

Target 1 Email:

Target 2 Email:

Natural Networking

Networking: most people hate it, yet it's key to maximizing your chances of landing great work. You've probably heard the often-used statistic that 80% of hires are made without a job posting; networking is a gateway to most of those hires. This is especially true for students. Since there are so many people applying to the same advertised roles, networking will allow you to have better chances for interviews, find many more open positions, and find roles that offer much more than more typical pathways of finding jobs.

An effective networker is one that makes new connections constantly, not only in structured networking sessions but also in the everyday experiences they have. We will explore both.

The Structured Session

Structured networking events rely on preparation and confidence, above all else. A prepared candidate is a valuable candidate, because preparation allows you to tell stories that demonstrate both your competence and interest. Not surprisingly, each trait is demonstrated best with a particular type of story. **Business** stories demonstrate your competence, and with it you talk about a time you accomplished a goal or excelled at a task. **Personal** stories demonstrate interesting traits or aspects of your life, such as elite-level competition, life-changing adventures, or memorable experiences that others would find fun. Together, these stories demonstrate the Competence and Interest of a high-value candidate, and with effective preparation, you'll demonstrate Confidence while delivering these stories.

In addition, if the situation permits, review the event guest list and choose three (or fewer) target companies to focus on. In total, plan to speak with 6-8 employees of these target companies. Throughout this section, these people will be referred to as "targets".

Exercise 8: Prepare Your Stories

(1) Use your resume or LinkedIn profile to determine two instances in which you demonstrated competence. Use each of these instances to create a **Business** story.

_____

_____

_____

_____

_____

_____

_____

_____

_____

(2) Create two **Personal** stories that demonstrate interesting aspects of your life.

_____

_____

_____

_____

_____

_____

_____

_____

_____

Note that as you continue to build your network, develop your experiences, and advance in recruitment, you may find it necessary to create more of these stories. The most prepared candidates will have ten of each type of story prepared in advance.

Building Social Capital at the Outset

Of course, you will not be able to fully demonstrate your value to 6-8 targets in the span of one or two hours. Therefore, the savvy networker will use their movement to their advantage. At the beginning of the session, spend fifteen minutes making quick connections with the 6-8 targets. At this stage, don't wait more than a minute trying to enter a conversation as it will be a waste of time. Instead, enter the circle at the target's right side, and rest your left hand on their right shoulder while offering a handshake with your right hand. You will need to wait for a slight pause in the conversation, and if you don't have this opportunity within a minute, move to another group.

After the introduction, there are two approaches that can keep the conversation short. If the target is already engaged with others, say "Hey, it's kind of busy right now so I'm going to circle back later because I'd really like to chat". If instead the target is open to conversation, engage in thirty seconds of small talk before saying "Look, I promised a couple other people I would chat with them, so I'm going to go say hello and circle back in a few minutes".

Pause and consider what these phrases imply: you're exceptionally well connected if you already know people here, not willing to waste time waiting on someone, and want to maximize the effectiveness of the session with several conversations. If you use the second phrase, it also shows that you keep the promises that you make, and trustworthiness implies competence.

In addition to how you portray yourself in this moment, you've given yourself an even better opportunity in that you will be able to rapidly connect with multiple people, from each target company, in only fifteen minutes. Not only will you now be able to mention the target's colleagues in conversation (to further demonstrate your connections), you'll also now have your choice of who to talk to, because your targets are anticipating your return. This anticipation will lay the foundation for an engaging conversation later.

Real Conversations - No More Small Talk

Once you have completed an initial cycle of introductions you will circle back to 4-5 targets to have longer conversations. Upon returning to the target, open the conversation with an AMP question: one that relates to Autonomy (their ability to choose at work), Mastery (their learning or skill development) or Purpose (their impact on their clients). These questions will draw a specific and detailed answer from the target. Some sample topics are listed below:

Autonomy: How they choose their projects/teammates/etc. and their favourite ones

Mastery: Lessons learned, continuing growth initiatives, feedback and development systems

Purpose: Significant project outcomes, personal mission, or barriers that were overcome

A list of 20 sample questions is provided in Appendix 1. With more practice you will learn which of these questions are most effective for the situation.

Since the target's response will be detailed, there will be several ideas expressed in what the target says. In fact, the more ideas, the better: you'll use one of these ideas as a connection to one of your **personal** stories. Therefore, take a mental note of the ideas that come up, and link one of those ideas to one of your stories. When sharing the story, be sure to link it back to the original idea, to clarify its relevance to the conversation and prevent the perception you're bragging. Keep in mind, you're only trying to demonstrate Confidence and Interest at this stage: the confidence to share something personal about yourself, and the trait or experience that makes you interesting and worth talking to. Build conversation around your story, and then link the story back to the original idea once more by asking one or two specific follow-up questions related to the target's first answer. With the target's answers to each of these specific questions, repeat the same process as before to share a **business** story. Again, make sure to link ideas explicitly, this time to justify your ability to do work that is like the work of the target. In this process, you will use no more than two of each type of story in the conversation.

Throughout the conversation two tactics may help you demonstrate more confidence. First, check your posture and stand tall with your feet firmly on the ground and your upper body open. Confidence is often undermined by crossing your legs while standing, or changing your stance often. For your upper body, stand with your arms away from your chest and your shoulders back, without pushing your stomach forward. A simple visualization is to look as though someone could easily punch you in the stomach and you would have no chance of blocking the punch.

Second, leadership is developed through the empowerment of others. Since you will be leading the conversation, show confidence and competence by getting opinions and answers from others in the group. Rather than keep the attention on the target for the entire conversation, move the attention to fellow networkers to demonstrate that everyone in the group is equal.

Exercise 9: Using Responses as Lead-Ins

Read each of the target's responses. After each one, write the transition that you would use to talk about your own stories.

(1) "Well, I wouldn't say we get to choose our projects so much, but I can tell my manager the initiatives I want to get involved in, and since our company is small enough I can help out anywhere that interests me – I do a lot of coaching and training"

_____

_____

_____

(2) "Lessons learned? I guess the biggest thing was to put the things that you learn into action. I mean, if you don't practice something how will you ever know if you can do it properly? That and sales. I had a really hard time learning how to sell our brand well"

_____

_____

_____

(3) "The thing is, everyone's going to have a different answer. I do this for the customers. It's great helping someone in a tough spot and they'll be thankful for the help you give them. I know it's just selling homes, but there's always a back story to it"

_____

_____

_____

Exercise 10: Conversation Practice

Take five minutes with a partner and practice linking key ideas to perpetuate the conversation. Aim to link the conversation such that you have no more than one "break" or awkward pause.

Close the Sale

While the conversation could go on forever this way, it's best to end the conversation after 8 minutes. This timing will allow you to use only your best and most relevant stories, and your initiative to end the conversation will further support your confidence, competence, and interest. If you want to collect the target's contact information (as in most networking conversations), ensure that you will bring value to them in your next interaction.

Put simply, if you ask for someone's contact information, you must have a reason for speaking to them again. Since you should always give more than you take in a relationship, have something to offer the target – this will also make them more likely to meet with you. This offering can be small and simple, such as a book or restaurant recommendation, but it must be of value to the target. Ideally, you will have hinted at this offer when the target showed interest in one of your stories.

Exercise 11: Bringing Value to the Connection
Use the space below to list at least ten items or information that you could offer your targets to facilitate closing the conversation.

Unstructured Networking

The design of structured networking sessions are intended to facilitate the atmosphere needed for networking; however, that atmosphere can often undermine the authenticity of the connections you create. The savvy networker will spend their time making connections on their own time, in any situation. The effectiveness of these conversations will depend on your confidence and your interest, as they have in other situations. Therefore, get involved with people who do things that you care about: Community organizations, sports leagues, and skill-building classes are a few examples. These initiatives allow you to put yourself in front of people with similar interests which then gives you more opportunity to make connections. Most conversations have five parts as follows:

1. Introduction and Small Talk – the opening to the conversation is dependent on the situation but can be as simple as "what brought you here?"
2. Value Story About Yourself – just like in a structured session, tell a story about yourself that links with the response of the other person.
3. Ask the Person's Motivations – ask a couple more questions to understand what they like to do and why. These motivations could be related to the situation or totally different.
4. Qualify the Person's Motivations – show your interest in the way they think or act, or the similarity between the two of you.
5. Ask for Information – once you've made a good impression you can ask for their contact information. Similar to structured networking, it is best that you have a reason, or something to offer, if you plan to meet again.

The best practice for this unstructured networking is to approach everyone regardless of age, sex, or appearance, and initiate conversation with them. Practice in all public settings for the most success and to build the greatest number of new connections.

The Recruitment Path

Humans invest in things that they see value in. For example, you buy a phone because you value its capabilities. You invest time into your job search because the result will bring you value. You invest time in other people because you see value in them. Your recruiters do the same – they invest more in you as they see more value in you. As in any healthy relationship, the key is to have equal investment from both sides.

While learning this system, you become more confident in your own value as a candidate, and, as a result, you should be looking for equal value from your next employer. Therefore, you will find it natural to begin to challenge and screen your employers in order to find a job that you value enough to invest in. This way, you build equal investment.

Investment on the Recruitment Path will almost always progress in the same manner, though different recruiters will take a longer or shorter time in each stage. The list below explains the different checkpoints that signal each stage, and the stages are included in the "My Targets and Tracking" sheet in the *OPERATION: JOB SEARCH* Tools Package. Your goal as a job seeker is to bring recruiters through each stage of the path.

1. Neutral – the company does not know you or is not yet interested
2. Meeting – people in the company are meeting with you, and talking about you internally
3. Accommodating – people in the company are doing little things for you at your request
4. Investing – the company is going out of their way for you, or is asking you for interviews
5. Courting – the recruiter is offering highlights and perks to convince you to work there
6. Finalizing – the recruiter is trying to finalize your recruitment through offers/negotiation

Note that these stages focus on the mindset of your counterpart – during the recruitment process, think about how the other person is thinking based on their actions, and use that to confirm which stage they have achieved. If an employee agrees to meet you, they must have reached the Meeting stage, at least.

The Interest Meeting (The "Airport Test")

When you agree to meet with an employee, you now have an opportunity to rove your value as a potential candidate. The first step is passing the "Airport Test", which is a simple question: "Would I want to be stuck at an airport with this person?" and it is definitely undervalued in its importance to your success as a job seeker. This is the first question that others in the company will ask after your meeting with the contact. Luckily, you are well prepared to demonstrate how interesting you are as a person based on activities earlier in this book. Remember, people would rather work with people that they like than with the smartest person in the room.

From your initial interactions with people at the company, you've set up this initial conversation to last only a short time, and you want the conversation to diverge as much as possible to topics other than work. This subtly replicates the airport-type conversation while keeping the pace fast and the topics interesting. Ideally, you will want to ask one (maximum two) AMP-style questions: the autonomy, mastery, and purpose questions that lead to elaborate answers. Just like your conversations while networking, link their answer to your stories, and use your stories to ask questions related to your story. Use an excited or energetic tone to build energy in the other person and appear both engaged and distracted, since this line of conversation will help you to stick with informal topics without it appearing to be intentional – after all, you are taking up the other person's time.

Especially during this first meeting, avoid the following subjects:

- Politics: disagreement will undermine the relationship, and politics are controversial
- Religion: similar to above as each person has slightly different beliefs
- Personal Finances: opens the door for negativity from either person and is personal
- Health: many people don't know how to respond to this topic which causes discomfort
- Relationships: similar to finances, relationships are personal risk negativity
- Gossip: most gossip is or leads to negativity, neither of which make you look good

If the other person brings up any of these topics, lead your answer with your vision or your values, and keep your answer both brief and positive. Immediately ask a mildly-related question to change the subject.

During this meeting you'll want to avoid checking your watch until you have used up almost all of the time for the meeting. If you check your watch well before this time, you'll need to ask another AMP question to restart the conversation. However, if you have less than ten minutes left, this is an ideal time to end the meeting using the following sequence:

1. Use an expression such as "Shoot" or "Oh gosh" to indicate surprise, then state the time and say "I'm sure you have other things to get to today. I should let you make your way, I have some other stuff I promised myself I'd finish today too. Well look, it was really great talking to you – really neat to talk about some of the non-work stuff too".
2. Allow the other person to state a response, and when appropriate, say "the way you talk about [their company] is really interesting. [Their company] wasn't on my radar as much before but I'm starting to consider it more seriously and I'm going to do some research. I might want to meet up again, would that be okay?"
3. Again, allow the other person to respond, and when appropriate, say "okay, well in any case, thanks for meeting with me today, I really enjoyed chatting with you. Good luck with the rest of your day".

Let's break this conversation down:

- In the first step, you've indicated a desire to stick to schedule, because both of you have other things to do today. This is indicating a respect for the other person's time as well as implying that you are busy too.
- Next, You give them a reputation for being great to talk to, and subtly reinforce that you are both interesting people.

- In the second step, You indicate a growing interest only because of what they had to say, which will make them think they are "winning you over" but that you had other plans beforehand. This promotes a more positive response when you ask to meet again and brings the relationship closer to the Accommodating stage.
- Finally, you subtly create ambiguity in whether you will reach out again, but maintain a high level of friendliness and respect for the other person. This will make the other person think and talk about you afterwards.

After the meeting, do some research on the company to understand, at a high level, the strategy and operations of the company based on public information. This will give you the information you need to ask about that person's division or department and understand their specific pain points.

The Competence Meeting ("Pain Points")

Every company has pain points. These are the aspects of the company that keep managers up at night, because they cause problems or prevent major opportunities. Your goal in the second meeting is to understand these enough so that you can pitch ideas for a solution. After you ended the first meeting, your research will generate a basic understanding of the company. You'll now want to request another meeting, and suggest that you have the meeting either at the office or somewhere very close to it. You can also explain that you've "done some research based on what's available but want to understand the real details". This phrase will help justify meeting in the office as well as the meeting itself. Request another half hour but (privately) plan that you could take up to 90 minutes.

The conversation in this meeting will be different than in the last: begin with something like this phrase: "I saw a lot of high-level information about [describe current efforts in the company], but I want to better understand how your day-to-day helps move something like this forward". This sets the expectation that the meeting will be specific to the other person's job. In most cases, they will start talking about their work; however, you might need to ask a more specific question for them to begin talking.

The immediate goal in this meeting is to find a significant pain point as quickly as possible, so some of the questions below might help guide the conversation in that direction:

- "So what part of the day-to-day work do you find the most challenging?"
- "Are there other departments that can, kind of, get in the way of that goal?"
- "Do you get caught on any roadblocks while trying to do that?"

Once you've identified a pain point, ask up to three questions to try to understand it better. When you think you understand the problem, mention a problem that you've solved before and explain how the two are related, even if the similarities are slight. Ask what, if any, solutions the team has tried, and once you've discussed them, offer the solution you used for your problem and explain how the two situations are different. This is an excellent opportunity to involve other people, asking "what do other people think about this? Do they have a couple minutes?"

When you meet others, make the first move and introduce yourself with your name, and explain that you are "starting to get interested in this company and am trying to learn more about things here". Make a point of introducing yourself to as many people as you can, including a hiring manager, and casually ask to tour the office as well. Involving many people in these meetings is a fast way to find the decision-maker for hiring in such a role.

Watch the reactions of others as you request more: if others comply with your requests, they are well into the Accommodating stage and might even be in the Investing stage. If this is the case, you can ask for a referral to the Hiring Manager at the end of this meeting. If others resist your requests, the third meeting will give you another opportunity to be referred.

There are two ways that you can solve the pain points while working at the company. The more obvious one is to be hired for that specific pain point, in which case the pain point is significant enough to constitute an entire position. More likely, the pain point is something you could tackle as a side project while in a different position. For example, an accountant at a small firm might work to improve training for new hires as a side project. You will want to choose one of these options (with a specific job title in mind) when you ask for a referral, framing the question similar to this: "I'm starting to understand a lot more and I think I can help as a [proposed job title] that works on some of the frustrations. It would be great if you could connect me with recruitment – what could I do to help the process?".

Regardless of whether you are able to ask for the referral, be cautious of time and overstaying your welcome. Be sure to thank everyone you met before you leave.

The Confidence Meeting ("The Proposal")

For some employers, this meeting is unnecessary, as you will have already started the interviewing process. However, this meeting provides one more opportunity to ask for a referral using your main contact. Set this meeting up, this time for fifteen minutes, and frame it as a follow-up to your last conversation. Again, plan to meet at the office or close to it: if you visited the office in your last meeting, propose the office again. Since the only goal of this meeting is the referral, jump into the conversation immediately and make minimal small talk. Say something similar to the following:

'So [Person's Name], you can probably tell I've gotten really interested in this company through our conversations. What you shared with me last time helped me to understand some of the frustrations too and I'd like to work on them a bit. I'm thinking that if I join as a [job title] I could help out with these things. What would you need from me in order to start the recruitment process?"

If they accept your request, write down each action item they specify for you, so that you can fulfill their requests within 24 hours.

At this point, you have maximized your chances of entering the interview process, but of course, this doesn't guarantee a referral. If your contact is not prepared to refer you, politely explain your disappointment and that you misunderstood the past interactions. Since you have many other companies that you are looking at, this is not a major loss to you. Make a few minutes of small talk and then thank the person for their time before leaving.

The Interviews

The first steps of the formal recruitment process are phone screens and interviews. Most phone screens can be successful using the techniques learned in the previous section: phone screens are designed to filter out candidates that are incompetent or unaligned with the company culture. Phone screens also follow a similar format with most companies. Interviews, on the other hand, will follow several different formats depending on the preferences of the company.

Behavioral

Interviews that ask for past scenarios are usually behavioral interviews. The best identifier of a behavioral interview is that the beginning of each question is along the lines of "tell me about a time that…".

While the possibilities of questions will seem endless, they can be grouped into only four types:

Working With Others

The majority of questions will relate to your teamwork and team leadership skills, since most companies think they operate in a collaborative environment. Interpersonal conflict resolution is viewed as an important aspect of teamwork. Sample questions include:

1. Tell me about a time you made decisions with a team.
2. Tell me about a time you had to address a teammate's underperformance.
3. Tell me about a time you had to make an unpopular decision.

Problem-Solving

Questions of problem solving will often relate closely to the **Business** stories that you've already prepared to demonstrate your competence. Your answers in this setting will be most effective if they focus heavily on the analyses you made to reach a decision, and why you chose those analyses in the first place. Sample questions include:

1. Tell me about a time you solved a problem.
2. Tell me about a time you worked under pressure.
3. Tell me about a time you had to handle a difficult situation.

Overcoming Setbacks

These questions are almost exclusively testing your resilience and adaptability. Overall, the interviewer wants to be sure that when things don't go your way, you aren't going to give up. In your answers, always provide an explanation of how you achieved success in the end, even if the interviewer doesn't ask for it. Sample questions include:

1. Tell me about a time when you failed.
2. Tell me about a time when you made a mistake.
3. Tell me about a time when the odds were against you.

Celebrating Success

Finally, some interviewers may simply ask about your successes. These are often opening questions to behavioral interviews, and are used to determine your excitement level as well as the tone for the rest of the interview. Positivity is a critical trait here, and you'll earn bonus points if you recognize others for their contributions as well as demonstrating your own accomplishments. Sample questions include:

1. Tell me about a time you worked with others to accomplish something great.
2. Tell me about a time you celebrated a victory.
3. Tell me about how you set goals.

The START Delivery Method

No matter the type of question, the answer should be delivered in the same method. The START acronym will help you remember each of the stages of the answer:

Situation

Open the question by describing the company or organization you were a part of and the initiative you were working on. It may also help to describe other people in the situation if they are relevant to the story.

Task

Be more specific about what you needed to complete. What would justify a job well done? What roadblocks were you facing? What constraints did you have on your course of action?

Action

Describe the actions you took. How did you decide what you needed to do? Did you set milestones or other goals? What analyses did you conduct in order to choose your course of action as the best one?

Result

Explain the outcome of your actions. Did you complete the task and satisfy your goals? Did the result satisfy everyone's goals? What metrics and statistics quantified the success or failure?

Takeaway

Explain what you learned from the experience and how it helps you to be more effective going forward. How could you do better the next time you're faced with a similar situation? How can you apply these lessons to other situations? How did you integrate the new information with what you already knew?

Exercise 12: Behavioral Interview Script

Use the START delivery method to answer the following question:

"Tell me about a time you overcame a failure and achieved success."

Case

The case based interview is one that features an open-ended business problem and finding the solution is typically led by the interviewee. A common flaw when practicing interviewee-led case interviews is that candidates focus on finding the answer when this is only marginally relevant to the outcome of the interview. In contrast, candidates should focus on only two aspects of their interviewing:

1. That the structure they use to sort the potential issues is both effective and logical
2. That they communicate their thinking and results in a clear and concise manner

Unstructured

The typical interview is unstructured and while it is the least effective, it is still practiced by the majority of companies. Any interview that doesn't follow the structure of the two types of interviews above can be considered unstructured. If an interview appears unstructured, conduct your responses in this format:

1. Begin by stating either your vision (what you want for the future) or your values (guiding principles that you use to operate your life).
2. Answer the question being asked based on your current situation or past experience.
3. Explain the exciting aspects of the job you are interviewing for, and how they allow you to move closer to your vision or better live your values.
4. Ask the interviewer a question about the job that relates to your answer.

An example question and answer is below.

"So [Candidate], I see you were on the executive team at the Investment Club during university. Can you tell me a bit about that?"

"Yes of course. As I've mentioned one of the major goals I have later in my career is to allow others to realize the full potential of their hard-earned savings, perhaps through my own fund. As part of the executive team I was able to see the pooling of resources in action and work with others to decide which assets we would invest in. We all learned a lot from each other including different types of asset classes which helped me to further diversify my own portfolio too. That's part of the reason I'm really excited for this job, because I'll get to learn from others and share what I already learned from the past. As I see how a larger investment fund operates I'll not only impact more people but also learn how to better structure operations to be effective on a larger scale. One of the questions I still have about this job is around the learning – how many other traders can I expect to work with each month?"

Exercise 13: Unstructured Interview Response
Use the format explained above to answer the following question:

"What are you involved in outside of work?"

When You Have the Offer in Hand

Ideally you will receive multiple offers around the same time period. Many offers, especially during on-campus recruitment cycles, will have a limited response time which is not only negotiable but also rarely enforced. Unless you identified multiple criteria during the interview process and all of these conditions have been met or exceeded, it is still in your best interest to negotiate before deciding on an offer.

Negotiation

The negotiation process does not begin with a phone call but rather with introspection. As you did at the beginning of this book, determine what you want out of a job, and what matters most. In a negotiation, you may be asked to make concessions and a strong understanding of the available tradeoffs will help you to make the best deal for yourself. For all aspects of the offer, determine both an aspiration (the ideal state) and a minimum outcome (the lowest you'll accept).

When you do call to negotiate, use a script similar to the following:

"Hi [Hiring Manager], I received the offer and I'm really excited to work with you. When I started looking for my next role my goal was to have [aspirations in outcomes that did not meet outcomes] because [vision or values]. Now, I realize that my goals are ambitious so I don't expect that we can meet all of them but I do want us to work together to find an outcome that we're both excited about"

Let's break this conversation down:

- You've reaffirmed your intention to work together. This is important to keep the other party engaged in the conversation.
- You've clearly stated your aspirations and linked your aspirations to your values or vision.
- You've explained that you are open to negotiation and you again explain that you want the outcome of the negotiation to work for everyone.

Decision

When you are finally ready to decide on an offer the process will involve the same introspection as you conducted in the previous section. Again, evaluate each of your offers with respect to your aspirations, and determine the tradeoffs between them to decide your optimal offer.

Operation: Job Search - Mission Accomplished

Maintain your Job Search Guarantee

For students using this booklet as part of the Operation: Job Search course with a Money-Back Guarantee, your continued efforts are necessary to keep the guarantee valid. The Operation: Job Search course guarantee is contingent on you completing the following:

1. Fill a post-course feedback form
2. Read both *Operation: Job Search* and *The Small Business Booklet* in their entirety, and submit a reflection on each to ensure your understanding
3. Use and submit the trackers to demonstrate your commitment to making one application per day, or otherwise making a significant advancement towards at least one possible job per day
4. Provide substantial evidence that you followed all recommendations made in the Operation: Job Search booklet, as recommended
5. Submit a weekly progress report to your Operation: Job Search course instructor

Further Reading
Appendix 1: AMP Questions

1. What was the most interesting project you've worked on in the last two years?
2. What was the most interesting initiative you've supported, outside of your core role?
3. Do you get to choose any of the things you work on? How does the selection process work?
4. Can you choose your teammates?
5. Do you prefer to work with people who are very structured, or less structured?
6. What kinds of events or initiatives do the teams do outside of work?
7. What have you learned so far at your job?
8. What do you learn at your job that you couldn't learn at school?
9. How do you get exposed to new challenges and industries at work?
10. How do you see your progression over time in your job?
11. How do you know when you're doing well at work?
12. What kinds of recognition does your company use to tell employees they are doing well?
13. What about your job makes you excited?
14. How does your job make you excited to get out of bed in the morning?
15. How would you best describe the impact your job makes on your customers?
16. How do you feel you've made an impact to your company so far?
17. What are some of the big changes you've helped with to make your company better?
18. How is your company creating value or making the world better?
19. How is this job setting you up for your dreams?
20. What do you learn at your company that you find useful outside of work?

About the Authors

Andrew Soave

Andrew Soave is the lead training facilitator and author of the Small Business Booklet, a guidebook for entrepreneurs and established small business owners to start and manage successful businesses. Aside from previous work as a management consultant, Andrew leads multiple small businesses and has founded a private equity practice under his flagship banner, Stallion Enterprises International Corporation. In this role, he is involved with several aspects of businesses including strategy, operations, marketing, employee training, recruiting, and engagement. Andrew is an experienced instructor in multiple settings and his expertise has been featured in blogs and workshops across North America. Andrew holds an MBA from the Rotman School of Management at the University of Toronto, a Lean Six Sigma Black Belt, and a BHSc from McMaster University.

Josh Arsenault

Josh Arsenault prides himself in his ability to train and facilitate job search and professional development in students and recent graduates. He has taken leadership positions in multiple organizations in recent years and focuses on improving hiring and training practices. Outside of these efforts Josh is a Senior Accountant at one of the largest financial services firms in Canada. Josh is a Certified Public Accountant and holds a Bachelor of Commerce from McMaster University.

Made in United States
Orlando, FL
08 March 2024

44538678R00024